CHARLIE BROWN'S CYCLOPEDIA

CLOTHES FROM HEAD TO TOE
What We Wear and Why

VOLUME · 14 ·

Based on the Charles M. Schulz Characters
Funk & Wagnalls

Charlie Brown's 'Cyclopedia has been produced by Mega-Books of New York, Inc. in conjunction with the editorial, design, and marketing staff of Field Publications.

STAFF FOR MEGA-BOOKS

Pat Fortunato
Editorial Director

Diana Papasergiou
Production Director

Susan Lurie
Executive Editor

Rosalind Noonan
Senior Editor

Adam Schmetterer
Research Director

Michaelis/Carpelis Design Assoc., Inc.
Art Direction and Design

STAFF FOR FIELD PUBLICATIONS

Cathryn Clark Girard
Assistant Vice President,
Juvenile Publishing

Elizabeth Isele
Executive Editor

Kristina Jones
Executive Art Director

Leslie Erskine
Marketing Manager

Elizabeth Zuraw
Senior Editor

Michele Italiano-Perla
Group Art Director

Kathleen Hughes
Senior Art Director

Photograph and Illustration Credits:
Animals Animals, 30; Craig Aurness/West Light, 29; The Bettmann Archive, 34, 43; David Celsi, 14, 21, 45, 47, 52; Comnet/West Light, 55; E.R. Degginger/Earth Scenes, 15; Ashod Francis/Earth Scenes, 53; John Gerlach/Animals Animals, 12; Giraudon/Art Resource, 17; Jon Gordy/West Light, 55; The Granger Collection, 35, 46, 51; Walter Hodges/West Light, 49; Pierre Kopp/West Light, 49; Bryce Lee, 26, 28, 39, 57; Zig Leszczynski/Animals Animals, 13; R. Ian Lloyd/West Light, 49; Terry G. Murphy/Earth Scenes, 58; The New York Historical Society, New York City, 23; Nick Nicholson/Image Bank, 49; Photofest, 59; Adam Smith Productions/West Light, 49; Michael R. Stoklos/Animals Animals, 33; UPI/Bettmann Newsphotos, 24; Brian Vikander/West Light, 54, 56.

ISBN: 0-8374-0061-9

Part of the material in this volume was previously published in *Charlie Brown's Second Super Book of Questions and Answers*.

Funk & Wagnalls, founded in 1876, is the publisher of *Funk & Wagnalls New Encyclopedia*, one of the most widely owned home and school reference sets, and many other adult and juvenile educational publications.

INTRODUCTION

Welcome to volume 14 of *Charlie Brown's 'Cyclopedia!* Have you ever wondered how cloth is made, or why queens wear crowns, or what a zoot suit is? Charlie Brown and the rest of the *Peanuts* gang are here to help you find the answers to these questions and many more about what we wear. Have fun!

CONTENTS

CHAPTER 1

A STITCH IN TIME
Cloth, Thread,
and Needles
..........12
Weaving
..........15

CHAPTER 2

CLOTHES OF
YESTERDAY, TODAY,
AND TOMORROW
The First Clothes 17
Pants for Men 19
Jackets, Ties,
Raincoats,
and Zoot Suits
....................20
Women's
Hoop Skirts,
Corsets, Pants,
and Pantyhose
....................22
Changing
Styles..........25

CHAPTER 3

WESTERN
DUDS
Native
Americans
.........28
Cowboy
Gear
.........31
Pioneer
Clothes
.........34

CHAPTER 4

ON YOUR MARK,
GET SET, GO!
Masks, Gloves,
Pads, and
Helmets
.............37
On the
Athlete's
Foot
...........40
Super Swim
Wear
...........42

CHAPTER 5

KEEPING
THINGS
UNIFORM
Knights in Armor
....................45
Soldiers in Uniform
....................47
Everyday People in
Uniform 49

CHAPTER 6

CLOTHES
AROUND
THE WORLD
Hats, Crowns,
and Wigs ...51
Veils, Sandals,
and Turbans
.................53
Dirndls and Kilts 54
Kimonos, Sarongs,
Muumuus, and Saris ...55
Getas and Bare Feet
..............57

DID YOU
KNOW?
.............58

People wear clothes for many different reasons. Charlie Brown wears a sweater to keep warm. Sally wears a dress with a bow because it makes her look pretty. Spike wears a hat to protect his head from the hot sun. Have you ever wondered how the first clothes were made? Let's find out!

A STITCH IN TIME

CLOTH, THREAD, AND NEEDLES

Who invented cloth?

No one knows. We do know that 5,000 years ago, Africans were already making cloth from tree bark. Before Columbus discovered America, Native Americans were also making bark cloth. It is possible that other people may have made cloth before either of these groups did.

To make bark cloth, both the Africans and the Native Americans used the same method. First they crisscrossed wet pieces of bark. Then they pounded the bark with rocks. The tiny fibers that made up the bark stuck together. They formed a piece of cloth. Some Africans still make bark cloth this way.

Who invented thread?

Thread is made naturally by worms, insects, and spiders. A spider, for instance, has special glands that make thread that the spider uses to spin webs. The thread is released through tiny organs in the back of its body called spinnerets.

The first human thread makers probably got the idea for spinning thread from spiders. First, though, the human thread makers needed fibers to make their thread.

A spider has special glands that make thread for webs.

What fibers are good for thread?

Fibers from any tall, stringy plant can be used to make thread. You can make thread yourself from tall grasses or cattails. Hang the plants in a cool, dry place for two or three weeks. They will become very dry. Then carefully pull apart the fibers and braid or twist them into thread. Flax, hemp, and cotton are three plants grown for their fibers. We make linen from flax fibers, rope from hemp fibers, and cotton cloth from cotton fibers.

The hair from these llamas can be used to make thread.

Could you make thread from your dog's hair?

You could if you had enough of it, but you'd need a lot of hair to make a piece of cloth. If your dog is shedding, you might sweep up the hairs and try it. However, your dog would be *very unhappy* if you tried to get some of its hair in any other way!

What animal fibers can be used for thread?

Thread can be made from the hair of any animal. People in ancient Asia used the hair of sheep, camels, and goats. Early South Americans used wool from wild mountain animals, such as llamas (LAH-muz), vicuñas (vye-KOO-nyuhz), and alpacas. These three goatlike animals still live in the Andes Mountains of South America.

Native Americans of North America used horsehair, buffalo fur, and moose hair for thread making.

I DARE ANYONE TO TRY TO MAKE THREAD OUT OF ME!

13

What is spinning?

Spinning is a way of twisting many fibers together into one long thread. For hundreds of years, people used a spinning wheel to make thread. It could spin only one thread at a time. Today modern factories use huge machines to spin hundreds of threads at a time. Here's how a thread is made.

The fibers are placed in a straight line. The end of each fiber overlaps the beginning of the next fiber. When the fibers are twisted, they cling together. The more the fibers overlap, the stronger the thread. Extra fibers can be twisted in to make the thread thicker.

ONE OF THESE DAYS, THIS WILL BE YOUR UNIFORM, SIR.

Who discovered how to make cloth from thread?

Probably fishermen in Egypt, 5,000 years ago, made the discovery. They made fish nets by knotting and tying threads. Nets were probably the first "cloth" made from thread.

Where did people get needles for sewing?

Before metal was discovered, prehistoric people carved needles from wood and bone. People who lived near the sea used fish bones and bits of shell. People in deserts used cactus spines.

Europeans were using metal needles about 2,500 years ago. Most Native Americans did not have metal tools before European settlers came to America just a few hundred years ago.

Prehistoric people carved needles from wood.

EAVING

Who invented weaving?

We don't really know. Weaving is a special way of putting together threads to make cloth. The process may have been discovered by net makers. Net makers tied the ends of their threads around weights. The weights kept the threads from getting tangled. The weights also made the threads hang tight and straight while the net makers were working. The idea for a loom may have occurred to someone who was watching fishermen make their nets.

A loom is used to weave some fabrics.

What is a loom?

A loom is a machine for weaving. The loom keeps a whole row of threads tight and straight. This thread, or yarn, is called the warp. Another row of threads can then pass under and over the straightened threads. This thread is called filling yarn in the U.S. and weft yarn in England.

15

CHAPTER 2

CLOTHES OF YESTERDAY, TODAY, AND TOMORROW

Snoopy never has to worry about what to wear. He always has a warm outfit! People throughout the ages, though, have always had different ideas about what kind of clothes to wear. So let's go along with Snoopy and see how clothing styles have changed over the years.

THE FIRST CLOTHES

What did the first clothes look like?

They were pieces of cloth or fur. People wrapped them around their waists, the way you wrap yourself in a towel. You've probably seen pictures of cave dwellers dressed this way. To keep warm, people wrapped other pieces of fur or cloth over their shoulders. Another early form of clothing was the tunic (TOO-nik). People in Central Asia were wearing tunics 5,000 years ago.

What is a tunic?

A tunic is a long shirt made of two pieces of fur or cloth. One piece is for the front, and one is for the back. The pieces are sewn together at the shoulders and at the sides. Tunics can be long or short. In ancient Greece, more than 2,500 years ago, men wore tunics just above their knees. Women's tunics reached to the ground.

In ancient Greece and Rome, men and women wore togas.

Did the ancient Greeks wear underwear?

A poor person in ancient Greece had only one tunic—which was both underwear and outerwear. A richer person wore a tunic as underwear, and a *himation* (hih-MAT-ee-on), or toga, over the tunic.

What is a toga?

A toga is a large piece of cloth worn over one or both shoulders. Togas were popular for many years in ancient Greece and Rome. An ordinary man's toga was smaller than a rich man's toga. A rich man wore his toga draped around his body several times. An ordinary man draped his only once. Togalike clothing is a style today in some parts of the world, especially Africa.

YOW, THE STREET IS HOT!

Most ancient Greeks went barefoot, even in the street!

In what other way did clothes show a person's wealth?

In ancient Rome, colors were the best way to know how wealthy a person was. Peasants were allowed to wear only one color, and usually it was brown or gray. The higher a person's rank was, the more colors he or she was allowed to wear. Colors also showed what a person did for a living.

How did colors show a person's job?

In ancient Rome, many jobs required clothing of certain colors. Here is a list of some of them.

purple, gold	royalty
purple stripe	high court official
blue	philosopher
black	religious leader
green	medical man

Some rich Roman women would wear several different colored tunics on top of each other. They would fold them so that all the different colors showed!

PANTS FOR MEN

When did men start wearing pants?

The first pants we know about were worn 2,500 years ago in Persia (now called Iran). Both men and women in ancient Persia wore pants.

The Persians traded with people from Central Asia. The Central Asians were nomads, people without settled homes, who lived in tents and moved from camp to camp. These nomads also wore pants. Today no one is sure if the Persians copied the style from the nomads or if the nomads copied the style of the Persians!

This drawing shows a European man wearing pantaloons.

What did men in other parts of the world wear before they wore pants?

After they wore tunics, men in Europe wore stockings and pantaloons. Pantaloons were wide, loose, short pants. The men also wore high boots and capes or long jackets.

Men in the 1600s wore high-heeled shoes and silk stockings trimmed with bows and lace!

When did long pants come into fashion for men?

Around 1800. Before that time, long pants were worn only by common workingmen. Rich men wore knee-length pants over stockings.

In 1789 a revolution began in France. The common people overthrew their rich rulers. After that, no one wanted to look rich. All men began wearing long pants.

JACKETS, TIES, RAINCOATS, AND ZOOT SUITS

When did men start wearing jackets?

The modern jacket came into use in England on December 15, 1660. Before then, Englishmen wore short capes. They copied the style from the French and bought many capes made in France.

King Charles II of England wanted his people to stop buying clothes from France. So on December 15, 1660, he appeared in court dressed in a Turkish-style jacket. He knew that everyone would copy his style and give up French capes.

The King of France was angry at Charles's fashion change. To get even, he made all the servants in the French court wear jackets.

20

Why were ties invented?

Ties were first meant to be like bibs. If a man dropped a piece of food, it would most likely hit his tie. The tie was easier to clean than a shirt. Eventually, men's ties became a good way to add decoration to a plain suit.

Who invented raincoats?

Raincoats were probably invented by soldiers, shepherds, and other people who had to spend a lot of time outside in bad weather.

Cloaks were the first rainwear. A cloak was just a flat piece of leather or heavy cloth. Its owner might have rubbed animal fat into the leather to make it waterproof. When rain began to come down, he simply threw the cloak over his head.

What are some unusual styles men have worn?

At various times, men have worn huge capes, very long feathers in hats, and tight starched collars. One unusual men's style of modern times was the zoot suit. It was popular with some American men in the 1930s and 1940s. The style called for a baggy jacket that reached to the knees and baggy pants that came up to the chest. The suit was usually dark-colored with thin light stripes. With it, men sometimes wore a long chain that hung from the chest nearly to the floor. The men usually put on suspenders to hold up the pants, and topped off their outfits with floppy hats.

ZOOT SUIT

Women's Hoop Skirts, Corsets, Pants, and Pantyhose

What was a hoop skirt?

A hoop skirt was a petticoat that looked like a cage. A woman wore a hoop under a dress or skirt. The skirt covered the "cage." The hoop skirt held the skirt out much as a metal frame supports a lampshade. Some hoop skirts folded up when women sat down.

When the style of huge skirts first became popular, women made their skirts stand out by wearing many petticoats at once. All those petticoats made it hard for women to get around because their clothes weighed too much. In the 1700s, women started wearing hoop skirts to lessen the weight.

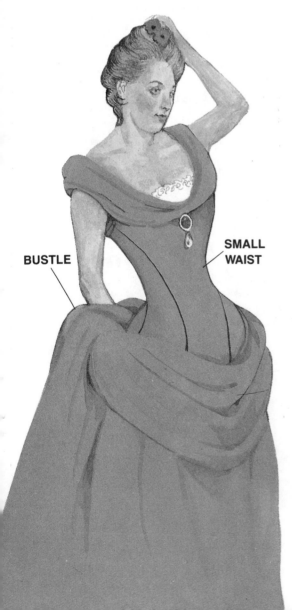

BUSTLE

SMALL WAIST

What is an hourglass figure?

From the 1840s until the early 1900s, people thought that a beautiful woman should have the shape of an hourglass. This meant that she had to be very small in the middle and wide above and below that. To help give themselves an hourglass shape, women wore either very full skirts or bustles. A bustle was a puff of cloth at the back of a skirt, often held up by a wire hoop. The hoop collapsed when the woman sat down. Women's waists were pulled in very tightly with underwear belts called corsets.

A girl began tightening her waist when she was about 14. Every morning she put on her corset— even if she was playing tennis that day! As the girl grew older, her corset was laced tighter and tighter. It kept her waistline from growing. A few women's waists were only 18 inches around! Most modern women have waists at least six inches larger than that.

In the 1800s, women wore corsets under their dresses to give them small waists, and bustles to help give them hourglass figures.

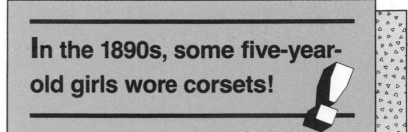

Amelia Bloomer

Wasn't it hard for women to breathe in tight corsets?

It certainly was. Corsets were both uncomfortable and unhealthy. That is why women began to talk about wearing more comfortable clothes. In 1850, Amelia Bloomer tried to get women to wear shorter dresses with roomy trousers—without corsets. People laughed at her idea and called her trousers bloomers, but Mrs. Bloomer won in the long run. About 50 years later, women got tired of being unable to move around. They started to wear simpler, looser clothes.

YIKES!

LET'S FACE IT, MARCIE. I JUST DON'T THINK CORSETS ARE FOR ME!

When did women start wearing pants?

In many countries of the world, pants have been part of women's clothing for hundreds of years. In Europe and the United States, pants for women were not considered proper until the 1920s. Movie stars helped make pants popular in America. The stars wore loose pajamas of shiny materials for lounging at home or at the beach. By the 1930s, women were wearing pants for sports and to parties as well.

Women wore "slacks" while working in factories during World War II.

While we were fighting World War II—from 1941 to 1945—many women worked in factories. They replaced men who had gone to war. The women factory workers wore overalls and other men's clothes. By the time the war ended, women were used to the comfort of pants, and began wearing pants more and more often.

During World War II, there wasn't enough silk for stockings. To make it look as though they were wearing stockings, women painted lines to look like seams on the back of their legs!

When were pantyhose invented?

Pantyhose became popular in the 1960s when miniskirts, very short skirts, became popular. Before then, women wore stockings that were held up by belts, called garter belts. These belts had hooks that fastened onto the stockings. Made of silk or nylon, the stockings were like long socks that came up to the thigh.

CHANGING STYLES

Why do styles change?

Styles are set by the people who design, make, and sell clothes. Ordinary people would not buy new clothes as often as they do if styles did not change.

Certain styles come and go very quickly. These styles are called fads. Fads sometimes are started in different parts of the country. For example, in California, where the weather is warm, people began to wear long colorful shorts called jams. Jams soon became popular all over the country. Movies and movie stars can also start fads. Lots of people will copy a style after they see it in a movie.

How have women's styles changed?

The lengths of skirts and dresses are always changing. In the 1950s, women and girls wore big skirts that hung below their knees. Circle skirts decorated with poodle appliqués were called poodle skirts. Styles became more daring in the 1960s, when miniskirts were popular. For a while, very long skirts, called maxiskirts, became popular, but when it rained, the bottom of the skirt would get wet! Women wanted skirts that weren't so long.

Today skirt lengths change from short to longer and back again almost every year. Women and girls can choose to wear just about any length, depending on what they find comfortable. Many women who have to dress up for work wear business suits with matching jackets and skirts.

In what other ways have styles changed?

In the last 50 years, many clothes seem to have gone back and forth between expanding and shrinking, without even being washed! Men's ties, jacket lapels, and pant legs have become wider and narrower, depending on the current style. In the early 1970s, some ties were so wide that they actually looked like bibs! Pant legs, too, went from being very narrow at the ankle to being very wide and floppy. These wide pants were called bell-bottoms. Today pant legs have shrunk back to a medium size.

Elephant bells are not something you use to call an elephant to dinner! They were pants that had such wide, flared bottoms that they looked like ringing bells as the wearer walked!

What will clothes look like in the future?

We don't know exactly what styles people will wear. Fashion changes in strange ways, but in the future we may wear fewer clothes. We probably won't need heavy winter coats because scientists in the space program have invented new types of cloth. One type is a warm, lightweight cloth used for astronauts' clothes. Some raincoats and other clothes are made of sturdy, lightweight cloth invented by space program scientists.

Some clothes in the future will probably be unisex. That means both men and women can wear them. Jeans and T-shirts are some of the unisex clothes that people wear today.

CHAPTER 3

Cowboys, Native Americans, and the settlers who moved west across the United States played a major role in how we dress today. Moccasins, vests, and cowboy hats are just a few of their contributions. So saddle up your horse with Sheriff Spike. He'll tell you all about Western clothes.

WESTERN DUDS

SHERIFF

NATIVE AMERICANS

What did the Native Americans wear?

Before the settlers came to America, many Native Americans wore leather tunics. In cold weather, they put on leggings—pieces of fur or leather which they wrapped around their legs. The leggings came up over their knees like long socks. Native Americans also wore soft leather shoes called moccasins.

Native Americans and early settlers sometimes kept their feet warm in winter by stuffing grass into the toes of their moccasins!

SURE BEATS COLD FEET!

How did Native American styles change after the settlers came?

After meeting European women, Native American women in the Northeast began wearing skirts and blouses. The fashion of cloth shirts spread among Native American men. In the Southwest, Native American lands were settled by people from Spain. Spanish men wore long pants made of cloth. Soon the Native Americans started to wear cloth pants, too.

How did Native Americans decorate their clothes?

Glass beads were a favorite Native American decoration. Native Americans would trade furs and blankets with the settlers for the brightly colored beads. They sewed the beads onto their tunics and moccasins and weaved them into their belts. Native American men also wore locks of hair on their shirts.

Colorful clothes and headgear were worn by Native Americans.

Did that hair come from people who were scalped?

Sometimes, but usually the men cut off some of their own hair or their wives' hair. Sometimes a Native American gave some hair to a friend who had saved his life.

29

What did Native Americans wear in battle?

Some fought in armor, a hard covering that protects a person in battle. The northwestern Native Americans made chest armor from thin strips of wood and leather. Around a warrior's neck was a wooden collar. It covered his chin and mouth, too. On his head he wore a carved wooden helmet. The helmet took the form of either a fierce-looking person or an animal. The human face was supposed to scare the enemy. The animal face was supposed to bring the warrior good luck. The wood protected the man from clubs and arrows.

Other Native Americans fought bare-chested. They protected their chests with shields. A shield is a flat piece of armor that a warrior carries on his arm. Native American shields were often made of buffalo skins. The skins were dried to make them strong and hard.

Did their chiefs wear huge headdresses to war?

No. It would have been difficult for a chief actually to have worn a headdress in battle. He wouldn't have been able to keep the feathers out of his way. Headdresses were called war bonnets because many of the decorations and feathers were prizes given for deeds in war. The bonnets were worn only for special ceremonies.

COWBOY GEAR

Why did cowboys wear such big hats?

The big domes and wide brims of cowboy hats kept the sun, rain, and snow off the cowboys' faces. Weather, however, was not the only reason a cowboy wore a hat. Cowboys didn't have cups or glasses out on the range. When a cowboy found a stream, he often put water in his hat and drank from the hat. Sometimes cowboys would bring water back to their horses in their hats.

Why were cowboy hats called ten-gallon hats?

Some of the cowboy hats were so big that they looked as if they could carry ten gallons of water. Of course, they couldn't. A hat would have to be awfully big to hold ten gallons, but the name stuck anyway.

What else did old-time cowboys wear?

When cowboys were working, they dressed in shirts and heavy work pants. If it was very cold, they added another shirt, not a jacket. Jackets made it too hard for the cowboys to move their arms. Vests also helped keep them warm.

31

Why do cowboys and cowgirls wear scarves around their necks?

The scarves that they wear are called bandannas. An old cowhand, J. Frank Dobie, once made a list of the uses of a bandanna. Here is the list.

1. Keeping the sun off the back of the neck.
2. Covering the nose on a dusty day.
3. Wrapping the ears in cold weather.
4. Tying on the hat in windy weather.
5. Blindfolding horses.
6. Wrapping a cut or wound.
7. Making a sling for a broken arm.
8. Straining mud out of stream water.
9. Covering the face of a dead cowboy.
10. Hanging horse thieves.

Today ranch hands probably use their bandannas for pretty much the same things—except, perhaps, hanging horse thieves!

Why do cowboys and cowgirls wear high-heeled boots?

High heels keep the feet of horseback riders from slipping out of stirrups. This is very important. Riders can easily fall off their horses if their feet aren't in the stirrups.

Where did cowboy styles come from?

Cowboy styles came to North America from Spain. The Spanish settlers brought cattle with them. They also brought cattlemen. Spanish cattlemen wore wide leather hats called sombreros (some-BRE-rows). They also wore leather vests, leather boots with metal spurs, and leather chaps.

What are chaps?

Chaps are heavy leg coverings that are worn on the outside of jeans or pants. They are made of tough leather and protect the cowhand's legs from thorns and cold when he or she is out riding.

Do modern ranch workers wear chaps?

Yes. People still wear chaps, but not as much as they used to. These days, cowboys in North America ride more often in cars or trucks than on horses. In South America, many cowboys still ride horses to do their work, so they still need chaps.

RIDE'M, COWBOY!

PIONEER CLOTHES

What clothes were in style for men of the Old West?

Wealthy men in the Old West copied eastern styles. They wore suits with matching long pants and jackets. With the suits, they put on fancy silk or velvet vests. They also wore white shirts and bow ties, and tall black top hats.

Most of the other people in the Old West worked the land. Because of this, they wore tough, rugged clothes that wouldn't be ruined by hard work.

WILD BILL HICKOK

WILD SALLY BROWN

Did pioneers ever wear Native American clothes?

Some men did. Wild Bill Hickok, a famous frontier scout and marshal, was known for his fancy Native American clothes. He wore tunics of soft leather embroidered with beads. He carried silver guns with ivory handles.

When were blue jeans invented?

In the 1850s, Levi Strauss began making heavy brown pants for the gold miners in San Francisco. Strauss put copper rivets in all the places where pants usually rip. This made them extra strong. Soon he began dying the pants he made blue. He called them blue jeans.

34

Levi Strauss first went to California to look for gold, but he ended up making much more money from selling pants than from panning gold!

What did women in the Old West wear?

A pioneer woman or girl usually wore a blouse and a long cotton skirt. She often had an apron to cover it, and when she went out, she threw a shawl over her shoulders. Sometimes in cold weather, women wore leather leggings like those of Native American women.

What did pioneer women wear to dress up?

A pioneer woman or girl usually had one good dress for going to church and to parties. One popular style about 100 years ago was the very full skirt. Pioneer women also tried to keep up with the latest styles from back East, which included the newest fashions in bonnets and shawls.

LUCY, MAY I HELP YOU WITH YOUR SHAWL?

CHAPTER 4

Shorts, T-shirts, sneakers, and sweat suits are clothes we wear for sports and other leisure activities. These clothes give a person lots of room to move, but some sports call for special outfits. Swimmers need bathing suits, baseball catchers need face masks, and scuba divers need flippers. Here are some of the special clothes that are needed for different sports.

ON YOUR MARK GET SET, GO!

MASKS, GLOVES, PADS, AND HELMETS

Do people ever wear masks in everyday life?

Masks are worn for many sports. Skiers sometimes wear knitted wool masks to keep their faces warm and to protect them from frostbite. Scuba divers and snorkelers wear masks to help them see underwater. Hockey goalies wear masks to protect their faces from flying pucks. Baseball catchers wear masks, too.

Why do baseball catchers need masks?

Catchers wear masks to protect their faces. A ball comes in very fast from a pitcher. If a batter hits a foul ball, it can bounce into the catcher's face. The mask stops it. Masks also protect the catcher from a bat that swings out of control.

What other protection does a catcher wear?

A catcher has a chest pad and shin guards. These serve the same purpose as the mask—to protect the catcher from fast balls and flying bats. A catcher also has a special padded glove called a mitt, which protects the catcher's hand.

37

What do the other baseball gloves look like?

For all positions other than catcher, the gloves have fingers that are sewn together. There is webbing between the fingers and the thumb. The first baseman's glove is much larger than those worn by other players because first basemen have to scoop up many balls off the ground.

What clothes do football players wear for protection?

In football, players wear helmets and pads. The pads are worn on their shoulders, ribs, hips, thighs, and knees. The shoulder pads have steel springs. Sometimes the leg pads are sewn into the pants. The pads help to protect the football player who is hit or knocked down.

What does a football player's helmet look like?

The helmet, made of unbreakable plastic, is padded on the inside. There is a bar across the front of the helmet to protect the player's face. Helmets have chin straps to secure the helmet. Players also wear mouth guards to protect their lips and teeth.

Did football players always have this much protection?

No. In the early days of football, they didn't have pads or helmets at all. The players wore pants and sweaters. The pants were made from heavy canvas. It wasn't until many players got hurt that pads and helmets were added.

What clothes do hockey players wear for protection?

Like football players, hockey players must be well-protected. Players wear gloves, leg pads, shoulder and arm pads, and helmets. Hockey helmets look a little different from football helmets because they don't have bars in front.

The goalie, the player who guards the goal area, has to wear extra protection. Stopping a fast hockey puck can be a dangerous job. To protect themselves, goalies wear heavy leg pads, chest protectors, and helmets with face masks. They also wear a special pair of gloves. One has a stiff board on the back to block flying pucks, and the other is a heavy-duty catching glove.

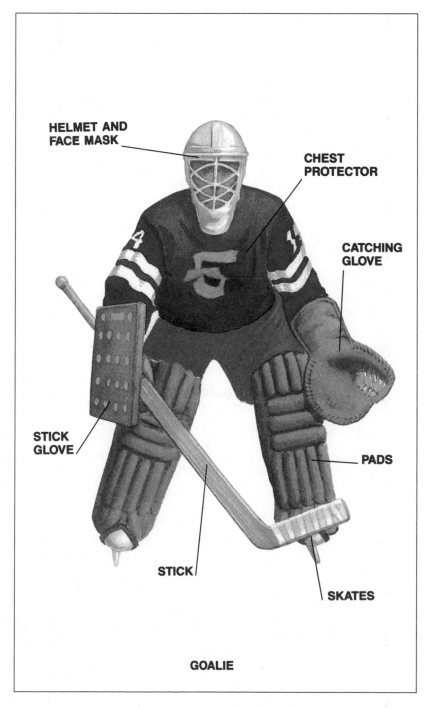

HELMET AND FACE MASK

CHEST PROTECTOR

CATCHING GLOVE

STICK GLOVE

PADS

STICK

SKATES

GOALIE

What type of shoes are worn for sports?

It seems as if each sport has its own special type of shoe. These shoes are designed to help the athletes play their sport better. Here are some of the different types of shoes for different sports.

Soccer—Soccer players wear shoes with cleats, or knobs, on the bottom. The knobs grip the ground, so the player doesn't slip.

Hockey—Hockey games are played on the ice, so hockey players must wear ice skates. Skates look like a high shoe with a thin metal blade attached to the bottom.

Scuba Diving—Scuba divers wear flippers. Made of plastic, flippers are large, wide, and flat, like a duck's foot. Flippers help divers move through the water fast.

Skiing—Skis don't just attach themselves to a skier's regular shoe. The skier needs a special boot. Ski boots are usually made of plastic with warm padding inside. The boots have a special place where they can attach to the skis.

Swimming—Swimmers go barefoot!

Golf—Golfers must keep their feet planted firmly in one place when they swing. For this reason, they wear shoes with metal spikes on the bottom.

Runners—Too much running can be bad for a runner's bones if he or she doesn't have enough cushion for the feet. This is why runners' shoes have thick rubber soles. Runners' shoes also are light so the runner doesn't have to lift up too much weight with each step.

On November 8, 1970, Tom Dempsey of the New Orleans Saints kicked the longest field goal— 63 yards—in football history. He had a special shoe made just for him because he has only half a foot!

SUPER SWIM WEAR

How do bathing suits help swimmers?

When cloth absorbs water, it gets heavy. Heavy clothing can slow a swimmer down or even make the swimmer sink. Today's bathing suits don't have very much cloth, and they are made of fabric that doesn't absorb much water. This type of lightweight bathing suit came into use only in the past 50 years.

What did the old-time bathing suits look like?

In the 1850s and 1860s, women on the beach wore suits with long pants, full skirts, and high collars. On their feet, they wore canvas bathing slippers. When all that clothing got wet, it was very heavy.

Little by little, bathing suits got smaller. About 90 years later, the bikini was invented. That barely covered anything!

What did old-time bathing suits for men look like?

Most men didn't wear special suits for bathing until about the 1850s. At that time, men and women started going to the beach together. At first, men wore just bathing trunks. By the 1870s, however, people were becoming more modest, so men covered up with knitted tops that were like T-shirts. Their trunks reached to the tops of their knees. This style lasted for about 50 years.

Men wore bathing suits like these in the 1890s.

What is a wet suit?

A wet suit must be worn in very cold water. It is worn mostly by scuba divers and surfers. A wet suit covers the entire body. It is made of rubber with lots of bubbles in it. The bubbles help the diver float. Wet suits are skintight, but they allow a tiny bit of water to leak in. The wearer's body heat warms up the water very quickly. This thin layer of water then keeps the body warm.

CHAPTER 5

KEEPING THINGS UNIFORM

Look all around you. Everyone seems to be wearing something different, but sometimes people wear exactly the same thing. When police officers, fire fighters, or airline pilots get dressed to go to work, their clothes are exactly alike. That's because they're wearing uniforms. If you play team sports or are a member of a scout group, you probably have a uniform, too!

KNIGHTS IN ARMOR

What is armor?

Armor is any protection that a person wears into battle. Most people think that, long ago, armor was made of metal, but sometimes it was made of wood or leather.

WHY DO I LET HIM TALK ME INTO THESE THINGS?...

Metal chest armor and helmets helped protect early soldiers from enemy arrows.

When did soldiers start wearing metal armor?

About 3,500 years ago. At that time, soldiers in the Middle Eastern countries of Assyria (uh-SIHR-ee-uh) and Babylon (BAB-uh-lun) sewed pieces of metal to their leather tunics. The metal gave warriors protection against enemy arrows. About 2,500 years ago, the Greeks wore metal helmets, and large pieces of metal on their chest and backs.

Much later, about 600 years ago, soldiers in Europe, called knights, began to wear full suits of armor. A suit of armor covered a soldier's whole body. Made of large pieces of metal joined together, the armor had hinges at the knees and elbows. A metal helmet covered the soldier's face, head, and neck.

What kind of shoes did knights wear?

Knights wore metal even on their feet. These shoes were pointy like the rest of the shoes of that time. The metal shoes were usually carefully fitted to the knight's feet.

How did a knight move around in all that armor?

He couldn't move very easily! Young knights had to train themselves to carry the extra weight, but their horses had the worst part of the deal. Knights rode horses into battle because that was the only way they could move quickly, so the horses had to carry the knight with all his heavy armor. Sometimes even the horses wore armor!

English soldiers 400 years ago used suits of armor such as this.

A full suit of armor—from helmet to foot pieces—weighed 55 to 65 pounds!

46

What did ordinary soldiers wear?

Until 400 years ago, most common soldiers wore leather tunics and helmets. Sometimes the leather was covered with small pieces of metal. In some countries, common soldiers wore chain mail under their tunics. Chain mail is a cloth made of tiny metal chains linked together. It protected the wearer from spears and arrows. Since the soldiers' tunics had no sleeves, only chain mail covered their arms. Some knights wore chain mail, too, but they wore it under a metal chest plate.

In the 1500s in Europe, some people slashed up their clothes to be in style. They copied this fashion from soldiers who had been in battle!

SOLDIERS IN UNIFORM

What do modern soldiers wear?

Today soldiers wear uniforms made of cloth. Each uniform has a name tag and a rank on it. Some have medals and patches on them. The color of the uniform shows what country the soldier is fighting for. For instance, in the Civil War, the Union soldiers wore blue, and the Confederate soldiers wore gray. The color of a soldier's uniform was important because no one wanted to mistake a friend for an enemy.

Are all the uniforms of one country the same color?

No. The color and style of the uniforms change with the different branches of the military. The four major military branches in the United States are the army, navy, air force, and marines.

What is a camouflage uniform?

Camouflage clothes are colored green and brown and gray like the plants, trees, and dirt outside. Such clothes help soldiers hide from the enemy. When a soldier is wearing camouflage clothes, the soldier will blend into the trees and plants in a forest.

What do the decorations on the uniforms mean?

Stripes, bars, and stars tell a soldier's rank—how important he or she is in the armed services. A beginning soldier may have a patch with one stripe. A longtime soldier may have eight stripes. Officers have bars and stars. A four-star general is one of the most important officers in the army.

Medals and patches also show what the soldier has done. Soldiers get different kinds of medals for bravery, special skills, and good service.

EVERYDAY PEOPLE IN UNIFORM

Many Japanese school children wear uniforms.

Do children wear uniforms?

Yes. Scouts wear uniforms. In most countries, children wear uniforms to school. In the United States, children who go to public schools don't wear uniforms, but many children in private schools do.

Are there other kinds of uniforms?

Yes. Here are some pictures of different people wearing uniforms. Their special clothing shows what kind of work they do.

Railroad conductor

Nurses

Police officers

Chefs

CHAPTER 6

CLOTHES AROUND THE WORLD

What you wear sometimes depends on where in the world you live. In different cultures and climates, clothes may have special meanings or purposes. Let's join the *Peanuts* gang for a quick fashion trip around the world to see special clothes from head to toe.

Hats, Crowns, and Wigs

Why do chefs wear tall white hats?

Chefs have been wearing white hats since at least 600 years ago. Back then, most Europeans wore special clothes to indicate their jobs. Bakers and cooks wore short, puffy white hats. Styles changed over the years, though, and in the 1900s, cooks started wearing tall white hats with puffs on the top. We now recognize the tall white hat as the sign of a restaurant chef.

Why do kings and queens wear crowns?

A crown sets a ruler apart from other people. A crown is a symbol that stands for power. Each crown has a design that represents its own country. When a country crowns its rulers, it gives them power over the country.

Kings and queens don't wear crowns all the time. Crowns are only for special ceremonies. Many crowns are heavy with gold and jewels. No person can wear one for very long without getting a headache.

Some of the clothes of King Henry VIII (the Eighth) of England had so many jewels sewn on them that no cloth showed through!

Why do lawyers and judges in England wear white wigs?

The English lawyer's wig is a style left over from 300 years ago. At that time, all important men in England wore wigs. The wigs had long curls that came down over the men's shoulders. When wig styles changed around the year 1700, lawyers and judges kept the older-style wigs as a sign of the importance of the law. In the 1790s, it was the style for men to put powder on their wigs. Some wigs were powdered white. Other wigs were light pink, silver, or blue!

Is it true that George Washington wore a wig?

No. People often say he did because wigs were in style for important men at the time of the American Revolution. Although many of the men who founded the United States wore wigs, Washington did not. He powdered his own hair and pulled it back in a ponytail.

Hair styles worn by rich women in the 1770s were almost three feet high!

Do people wear wigs today?

Yes. Sometimes actors wear wigs to look more like the characters they are playing. Other people wear wigs because they have lost their own hair. Modern wigs look very much like real hair. Wigs worn by men to cover bald spots are called toupees (too-PAYS).

Veils, Sandals, and Turbans

Why do women in some countries wear veils?

Veils are supposed to keep men from seeing women. This custom is very old. Women were wearing veils in a Middle Eastern country called Ur as far back as 5,000 years ago.

A few religions forbid women to show their faces. Some women who belong to the Muslim faith cover every part of their bodies except their eyes.

Do any men wear veils?

Yes. Among the Tuareg (TWAH-reg) people of the Sahara Desert, all men cover their faces. Women go without veils. Tuareg men believe that they are special, so ordinary people may not see their faces. Tuareg men wear veils even when they eat and drink!

Loose clothes help keep people cool in desert climates.

What else do people in the Sahara Desert wear?

Tuareg people wear sandals with big, wide soles shaped like paddles. The wide soles keep their feet from sinking into the sand.

They also wear what most desert people wear—loose clothes. Loose clothes allow air to reach a person's body easily. The air helps to keep the body cool. Some desert people dress in long, flowing robes. Others wear loose shirts and trousers.

Sahara Desert dwellers protect their heads from the sun by covering them with cloth or wrapping them in turbans.

What is a turban?

A turban is a long piece of cloth that is wound around a person's head. Men wear turbans in Egypt, India, Saudi Arabia, and other Asian and African countries. In some African countries, women wear turbans.

Wrapping a turban is like tying a huge knot, with your head at the center. You pass the ends of the turban over and under each other. Then you tuck the ends of the turban under the folds of cloth.

There are hundreds of different ways to wrap a turban. The way one is wrapped sometimes shows what tribe the wearer comes from.

Turbans are worn by many men in Asia and Africa.

Some Asian and African men wear modern shirts and pants, but still wear turbans!

DIRNDLS AND KILTS

What is a dirndl?

A dirndl is a brightly colored skirt that used to be worn by peasant women in Austria. Now makers of children's clothes have copied the style, and many girls' skirts and dresses are made in the dirndl style. The skirt is very full, and it is usually embroidered at the bottom. It is pulled in tight at the waist. A white apron is often draped over the front.

Do any men wear skirts?

In a few countries, men sometimes wear skirts. These styles have been worn in their countries for hundreds of years.

For special occasions, some Scottish men dress in knee-length skirts called kilts. Kilts are woven in brightly colored plaids. Each Scottish plaid belongs to a different family, or clan.

The guards at the Greek parliament building also wear kilts. The Greek kilts are white.

Kilts are part of traditional Scottish dress.

KIMONOS, SARONGS, MUUMUUS, AND SARIS

What is a kimono?

The kimono is the traditional dress of the Japanese people. It is a long robe with wide sleeves and a wide sash. It is usually decorated with many beautiful designs and colors. Both men and women wear kimonos, but these days, they are worn only on special occasions.

What is a sarong?

A sarong is a long piece of cloth that is wrapped around the body once. People who live on islands in the Pacific wear sarongs. So do people of Southeast Asia. Men wrap their sarongs at their waists. Women wrap theirs under their arms.

Some people in Africa wear clothes that look very much like sarongs.

What is a muumuu?

Some women in Hawaii wear long, loose cotton dresses called muumuus (MOO-mooz). The style began when settlers arrived in Hawaii in the 1800s. They thought the Hawaiian women weren't wearing enough, so they made them cover up with muumuus.

ALOHA, SWEETIE.

What is a sari?

A sari is a long piece of cloth worn by women in India and neighboring countries. It is usually made of silk or some other thin material. Before dressing in a sari, a woman puts on a short blouse and a half-slip. She tucks one end of the sari into the slip and wraps the other end around her body a few times and then puts it over her shoulder. The bottom of the sari reaches the floor.

A young Indian girl in a brightly-colored sari

GETAS AND BARE FEET

What do Eastern people wear on their feet?

In China, Japan, and other East Asian countries, people wear shoes like ours, but rope or straw sandals are also popular. One style of Japanese sandal is called a *geta* (GEH-tah). A *geta* has a thick wooden sole. In cold places, such as Tibet and Mongolia, people wear boots of fur or heavy cloth.

People who live on the Pacific Islands often go barefoot since the weather is warm.

What do African people wear on their feet?

What they wear on their feet depends on where they live and how much money they have. Jungle dwellers go barefoot. Others, too poor to buy shoes, also go barefoot. Some people can afford sandals. In African cities, many people wear Western-style shoes. Western-style means similar to clothing styles that come from modern Europe or America, parts of the world called the West.

Are there people who don't wear any clothes at all?

Only a very few of the world's people go naked. They live in isolated parts of Australia, South America, and Africa. They belong to tribes that have not met many people from other places. However, people who wear no clothes decorate their bodies with paint and dress up in colorful jewelry for special occasions.

About 300 years ago, some European women wore shoes with platforms up to 30 inches high!

GUESS WHO?

Behind the Mask

Lots of children wear masks when they go trick-or-treating on Halloween every year. Modern kids aren't the first people to wear masks, though. More than 10,000 years ago, cave dwellers in Europe wore masks. Before a hunt, they held special dances. They believed the dances would help them have a good hunt. At the dance, they wore masks of animals they were going to hunt.

Don't Sneeze in That Suit!

Because the space suits worn during early space flights were pressurized, astronauts could not touch their faces with their hands. This made it impossible to blow their noses! To scratch an itch, astronauts would have to rub the itchy part of their faces against the inside of their space helmets.

Now astronauts inside the space shuttle wear everyday clothes. This lets them do all the things in space that they do on Earth—like scratching their noses.

Rings and Things

People in almost every culture wear jewelry. Metal and stones are worn on earlobes and around necks, fingers, wrists, and arms! Sometimes the jewelry serves a purpose. For example, the Paduang women of Burma stretch their necks by wearing fitted brass rings around them. You might wear a bracelet made of woven threads as a sign of friendship. Jewelry can be as simple as a beaded necklace or as valuable as a diamond.

Colorful jewelry is worn by women in Africa.

Pointy Toes

During the Middle Ages, shoes with pointed toes became very fashionable. The toes of pointed shoes became so long they flapped when a person walked! By the fourteenth century, pointed shoes sometimes went almost 12 inches beyond the wearer's real toes! Poor people were allowed shoes with toes no longer than 6 inches.

Boys in Skirts

As recently as 200 years ago, most boys in Western countries wore full-length skirts! They dressed this way until they were about six years old.

The Ruby Slippers

The famous shoes worn by Dorothy in the movie *The Wizard of Oz* were sold for $165,000 at an auction in 1988. The ruby slippers are size 6B.

IN THE NEXT VOLUME

Have you ever wondered when people first tried to fly, or who the Red Baron was, or how a heavy airplane stays up in the air? You can find the answers to these questions and lots more in volume 15, *Planes and Things That Fly—Up, Up, and Away.*

POOF! POOF! POOF!

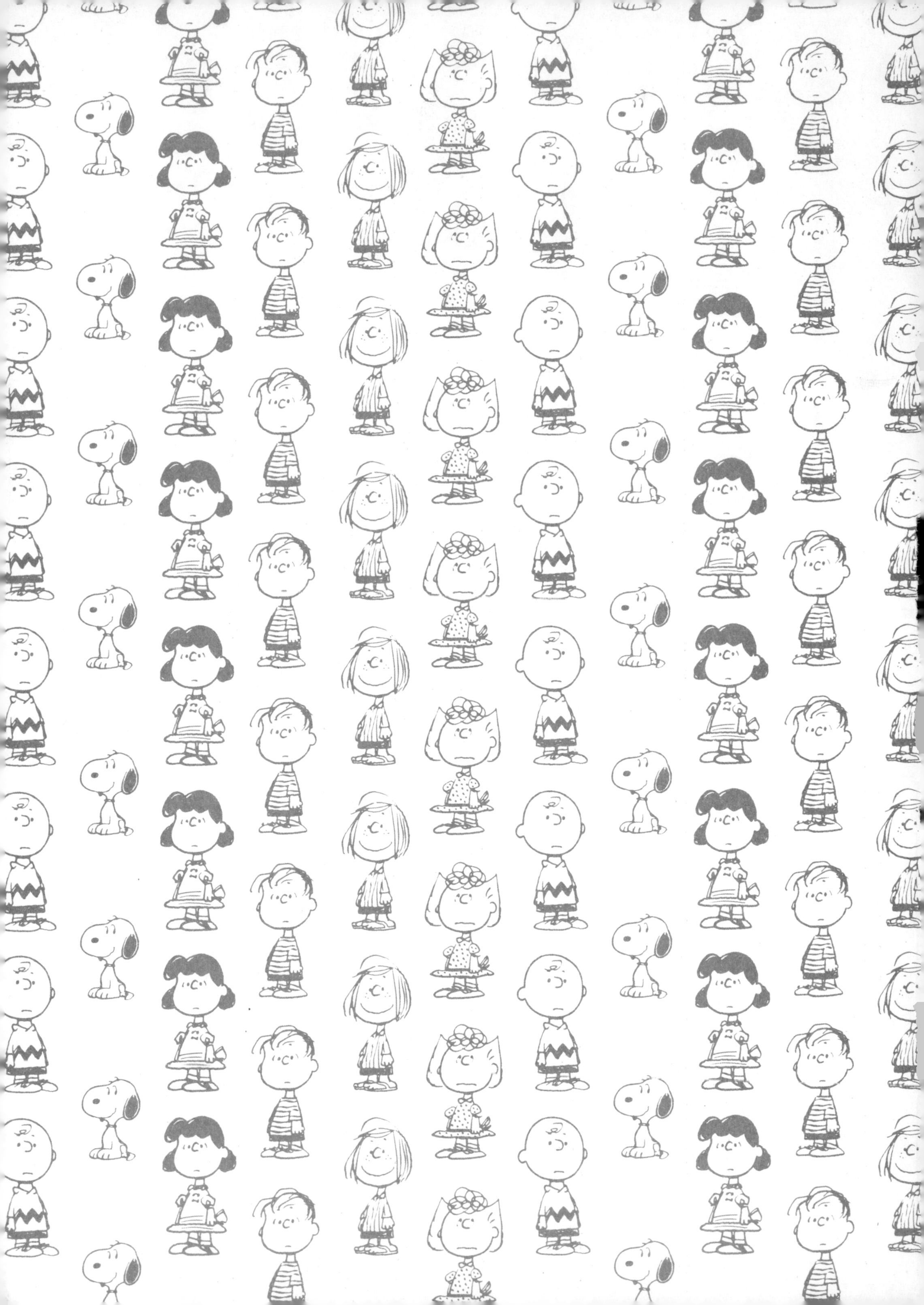